I feel loved!

I feel calm.

I'm feeling EXCITED!

All about Feelings

I feel sad.

I'm feeling happy.

We're feeling friendly.

We're feeling silly!

I'm not sure how I feel.

I'm feeling cross.

Contents

Usborne

All about Feelings

Felicity Brooks
and Frankie Allen

Illustrated by Mar Ferrero

With thanks to Holly Docherty
BEd Primary and SENCo

I felt **proud** to illustrate this book!

I felt **happy** to write it!

I felt **excited** to design and help write this book!

Everyone has feelings

How are you feeling today? Happy? Hungry? Maybe you're feeling sad? Everyone in the world has feelings all the time, but the way that we show them changes as we grow.

Tiny babies can't talk or even smile. They can only show how they're feeling by crying (or not crying). This means it can be hard to work out what's wrong.

WAAAAAAAA!

Is she hungry?

She could be tired.

I think she wants a cuddle.

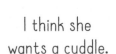

Mine!

Noooo! Mine!

Oh dear!

NO WANT SHOES!

Toddlers are good at showing feelings, but don't understand why they have them. And they don't know that other people (and pets) have feelings too.

Older children are also very good at showing feelings and may learn
to tell how other people are feeling by looking at their faces.

How do you think these children are feeling? Can you match the words and faces?

angry   excited   nervous   calm   happy

sad   proud   grumpy   worried

Can you think of a time when you felt any of these feelings?

Body messages and clues

Your body has ways of showing feelings, too. Some are messages to tell you that your body needs something.

Tara is feeling TIRED.

Isaac is feeling ILL.

Hannah is feeling HUNGRY.

Holly is feeling HOT.

Theo's feeling THIRSTY.

Connor is feeling COLD.

Can you tell these children what they need to do to feel better?
Match a speech bubble to each child.

Eat some food.

Take off your sweatshirt.

Take a nap.

Drink some water.

Tell a grown-up. You might need some medicine or a doctor.

Put on some warm clothes.

Our bodies can also show feelings that are inside our heads.
See if you can work out how these people might be feeling
just by looking at their body clues.

Hee hee!

Anya is smiling and
laughing loudly.
How is she feeling?

Oscar is crossing his
arms and sticking
out his lower lip.

Mrs Butler has a red
face. She's shouting and
stamping her feet.

Sob!

Ash has gone very
quiet, and he is
starting to cry.

Sandeep won't look at
anybody and wants to
run away and hide.

Maria's all jumpy and
can't sit still. She is
breathing fast, too.

Next time you are out and about, take a look at some of
the people around you. Can you tell how they are feeling?

So, how are you feeling?

It can be hard to answer this question and to give your feeling a name, but saying what it feels LIKE can help. You could even give your feeling a COLOUR.

"I feel like there's a volcano with

HOT, RED FLAMES

inside me, ready to

EXPLODE"

BUZZ BUZZ

"It feels like there's a load of wasps buzzing around my head."

I want to STOMP like a dinosaur . . .

Arghhhh!

. . . and YELL!

Rarrrrrrrr!

And ROAR like a tiger.

I am feeling ANGRY. My colour is RED.

"I feel like I'm sliding down a rainbow!"

Weeeeee!

"It feels like I'm running through a field of flowers and swimming in sunshine."

Ooo! I just want to give you a huge hug!

Ha ha!

I want to PLAY ...   ...and JUMP.   And HUG everyone!

I am feeling HAPPY! My colour is YELLOW.

"I feel like there's a

HEAVY GREY CLOUD

above my head."

"It feels like I'm all alone in the middle of a cold, blue lake."

Sniff!

Sob, sob!

I want my mummy.

I want to SIT ALL ALONE …

… and CRY.

And CURL UP INTO A BALL.

I am feeling SAD. My colour is BLUE.

"I feel like a sleepy cat stretching out in front of a fire, purring softly."

"I feel like my blanket is **hugging** me."

I want to SING quietly...   ...and S-T-R-E-T-C-H.   And WIGGLE my toes.

I am feeling CALM. My colour is GREEN.

Why, why, why?

Feelings inside our heads usually happen for a reason. These children and their teacher are talking about how they are feeling and saying why they think they feel the way they do.

I'm feeling a bit upset because I've lost my pencil case.

I'm feeling calm and **happy** because I love drawing.

I'm feeling **sad** today because my grandad is ill.

I'm feeling annoyed because her picture is better than mine.

I'm new here and I'm feeling **shy** because I don't know anyone yet.

I'm feeling **excited** because it's my birthday party this afternoon.

Think about how you are feeling right now. Can you give your feeling a name? Can you say WHY you feel that way?

How would you feel?

Choose words from the clouds to say how you think you would feel if these things happened to you.

You can choose as many words as you like.

sad worried lonely
upset bored disappointed

proud cheerful
happy brave
excited

You're waiting for your turn to go on an enormous water slide for the first time. How would you feel?

At home-time, all the other children have been picked up but no one's come for you yet. How would you feel?

He's late, again!

You're cuddled up in bed with your best toy, listening to a really good story. How would you feel?

Bedtime!

You want to carry on playing a game but your mum says you have to go to bed. How would you feel?

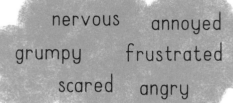

kind   relaxed

calm   helpful

nervous   annoyed

grumpy   frustrated

scared   angry

Your teacher just told you that you got the part you wanted in the school play. How would you feel?

You're playing with your friend. All of a sudden her dog runs over the board and ruins your game. How would you feel?

You've heard that your grandma has been taken into hospital and your dad's looking worried. How would you feel?

Your teacher just read a story that you wrote and said that it's really good. How would you feel?

Changing feelings

Feelings can change through the day, so you don't always have to get stuck with a feeling you don't like. Here's Lara's day. How do you think she feels in each picture?

RAAAAAAR!

Gerofff!

Yipee!

1 Lara's brother jumped on her bed and made loud dinosaur noises to wake her up.

2 Lara's dad made everyone pancakes for breakfast.

You smell lovely!

Oh no!

6 They went to see Grandma and she gave Lara a big hug.

7 On the way home, Lara's water bottle was empty.

Oh that's a shame!

8 At home, her mum got a message to say Lara's friend couldn't come over to play.

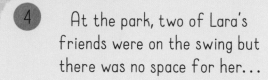

3 On the way to the park, Lara fell over and grazed her knee.

4 At the park, two of Lara's friends were on the swing but there was no space for her...

Woo hoo!

Thank you!

5 Lara's brother gave her a pretty leaf he'd found.

...so Lara went down the big slide by herself for the first time.

Yawn!

Thanks, Dad!

9 Her dad gave her a lovely new picture book to read.

10 After a busy day, she nearly fell asleep reading the book.

Think about what you did today. Did your feelings change?

Jumbled up feelings

We don't always feel just one thing at a time. When feelings are mixed up, or even opposite, it can be confusing. But everyone has jumbled up feelings sometimes.

When your teacher gives you a special certificate, you might feel a bit EMBARRASSED but also PROUD.

You might feel HAPPY to see pictures of your friend's holiday but also SAD as you didn't go too.

You might feel very EXCITED about learning to swim, but also a little WORRIED about trying a new thing.

When your friend is being mean, you might feel ANNOYED but you still feel FRIENDLY towards her.

If your pet died, you would feel SAD but perhaps also ANGRY because you wanted it to stay alive.

After a running race, you may feel EXHAUSTED and out of breath, but HAPPY that you finished.

Sometimes body messages can get jumbled up with feelings that are inside our heads. That can be extra confusing!

When was the last time you ate?

I'm NOT tired!

My tummy hurts!

Sometimes you can feel ANGRY because you are HUNGRY.

Sometimes you can feel GRUMPY because you are TIRED.

Sometimes you can feel SAD because you are ILL.

It's OK if you can't work out why you are feeling the way you do. Sometimes our brains make us feel something for no special reason.

Talking about feelings

Other people can't always tell how you are feeling just by looking. And you can't always tell how they're feeling either. That's why TALKING about feelings is a fantastic thing.

Talking can help you understand your feeling and give it a name:

Sharing feelings can help you find ways to solve problems.

Talking about feelings can help you get on with your friends.

When you DON'T talk about unhappy or angry feelings, they can get bottled up inside you like a fizzy drink in a bottle. These fizzy feelings can EXPLODE out in ways that hurt or upset other people, or hurt you.

But the good news is you DON'T have to get stuck with fizzy feelings, and you don't have to EXPLODE and upset or hurt people or break things. Take a deep breath and turn the page to find out more.

Take a moment

Feeling angry, upset, frustrated or sad can make you want to shout, scream, cry or even hit out. But there are things you can do instead.

1. Start by closing your eyes and taking a really deep breath.

2. Then, let the breath out very slowly, counting to ten in your head.

Then to let the feeling out, you could . . .

BANG on a pan.

Hug yourself.

Go to a quiet place.

Run really fast on the spot.

Dance to loud music . . .

If you're angry and you know it, stamp your feet.

. . . or stamp around and sing at the top of your voice.

And if you don't feel any better, you could . . .

Squash and squeeze some modelling clay with your hands.

Scribble a picture of your feeling, then screw it up and throw it away.

. . .and then I felt really cross because she pushed me.

I understand how that could make you feel cross.

Or you could . . .

TALK TO SOMEONE and tell them all about it.

If you don't like what you are feeling, talking can really help you feel better and even change the way you feel.

Feeling worried?

Here are some ideas for things you could try if you are feeling worried about something.

It's OK.
It's OK.
It's OK.

Tell yourself 'it's OK' until you feel better.

Imagine you are a cat taking a nap. Close your eyes and relax.

Ha ha!

Watch a programme or film that you love.

I love this page!

Look at a book you really like.

Cuddle your favourite toy and think of a peaceful place.

Imagine floating down a stream, away from all your worries.

Tell someone all about it ...

Writing and drawing is a really good way of helping with feelings. You could even write a feelings diary and add some little drawings.

Me!

	My day	How I felt
		Silly
Monday	Dropped my book bag on way to school – all covered in mud.	
Tuesday	Played with Joshua at lunchtime.	Happy
Wednesday	Got told off for breaking crayons but it wasn't me.	Frustrated
Thursday	Josh played with Aran at breaktime.	Left out
Friday	Played a brilliant game with Josh AND Aran.	HAPPY!!!
Saturday	Excited because it's Aran's BIRTHDAY PARTY TODAY!	Excited!
Sunday	Pouring with rain. Football cancelled.	Fed-up

Making choices

Nobody can help their feelings and there's nothing wrong with showing them. But when you have a feeling that you don't like, you can CHOOSE how you show it and what to do with it.

Which do you think are good choices for each of these feelings?

You feel **sad** because your friend is going to another school. What do you do?

Make someone else feel sad too.

Sulk and cry.

Tell your friend how much you will miss her.

Find out how you can keep in touch.

 Talk to someone about how you feel.

You feel **upset** because your friend has a new hamster and you aren't allowed a pet. What do you do?

Does she eat carrots?

Scream and shout.

Read a book about hamsters.

Ask if you can help your friend take care of the hamster.

Pretend that you hate hamsters.

 Talk to someone about how you feel.

You feel **disappointed** because your friend is ill and can't come for a sleepover. What do you do?

Make your friend a get well card.

Ask if your friend can come another day.

Scream and shout and kick the bed.

Tell your friend you don't like him anymore.

Talk to someone about how you feel.

You feel **scared** because your bedroom is dark at night. What do you do?

It's OK. I understand that you're feeling scared.

MUM! I feel scared.

Shall we try a nightlight tonight?

Ask if you can have a nightlight.

Cry yourself to sleep.

Cuddle a toy and tell yourself it's OK.

Refuse to go to bed.

Talk to someone about how you feel.

Did you notice there's one choice that's the same for every feeling?

Talking to someone you know well about how you feel is ALWAYS a good choice. It could be a parent, a carer, your teacher or your friend.

Helping friends and family

Thinking about how other people are feeling and trying to help them can make you feel good. One way of helping is to imagine how you'd feel if you were the other person. Then, think how you'd like people to treat you.

Can you think of any times when you have helped people and made them feel better?

Being kind to yourself

We know it feels bad when people are mean to us, but sometimes we're mean to ourselves and this can make us feel unhappy, too.

Next time you're being mean to yourself (having unhelpful thoughts), try to turn your thinking into something more kind and helpful, like this:

I'm never going to be as good at singing as my brother.

I don't have to be good at everything and I still enjoy singing.

I didn't win the race. I am hopeless at EVERYTHING.

I may not have won, but I tried my best and I'm good at other things.

I'm last in the queue. It'll be ages before I get a drink.

I'm with my friend and we can chat and tell jokes while we're waiting.

It's all my fault she got hurt. I suggested this game.

It was an accident. It's nobody's fault.

Everyone sometimes gets stuck with a difficult feeling or lets fizzy feelings explode. But remember that difficult feelings do pass and it's OK to ask for help if you need it. Dealing with feelings gets easier the more you talk about them.

Some notes for grown-ups

How are you feeling today? Being able to ask and answer this question is a key stage in children's development and important for maintaining good relationships, effective learning, and good mental health. Children who don't learn to process and manage feelings well can get 'stuck' emotionally and may find it hard to deal with everyday challenges.

This book is designed to help children recognize, understand and name different feelings and to learn to talk about and manage them in helpful ways. There are many things that adults can do to encourage this, so remember that:

• Learning skills for managing feelings takes time and practice.

• Noticing and being able to name feelings comes first.

• Understanding and being able to express what has caused a feeling is important.

• Talking about everyday feelings in normal conversations makes it easier when difficult feelings come up.

• Children can't help their emotions and they're important and real to them, so don't ignore or deny their feelings or immediately try to divert attention away from them.

• Children need time to recover after an 'explosion' and some take much longer than others. (Such episodes can make children very thirsty, so offering a drink will help.)

• It's usually best to talk about difficult feelings when things have calmed down and everyone's more relaxed.

• Using colours to describe or indicate feelings can help children who choose to be or are non-verbal. You could put up a colour chart or give your children cards which they can show you.

• Children acquire these skills in different ways and at different stages, so don't compare your children. Remember that the same event may evoke a different emotion in two different children.

Things to try at home

• Use feelings words in everyday conversations: "It's disappointing that Alex can't come over today."

• Learn to recognize 'triggers' for your children and help them with strategies for when they feel difficult emotions building. (Go to a safe place, get a fiddle toy, hug their teddy . . .)

• Invite children to describe their feelings: "I'm feeling really sad that Tiddles died. How about you?"

• Acknowledge and validate your child's feelings using statements such as "I can see that you're feeling annoyed. I'd feel annoyed too if that happened to me."

• Remind children often that they can make a choice about how to respond to a feeling.

• Coach them in coping strategies such as taking deep breaths, counting slowly to ten, etc. (See pages 22-25).

• Help older children learn to eliminate negative self-talk and reframe their thinking (as shown on pages 30-31).

• Read all kinds of stories to children, not only happy ones. Talking about difficult emotions in books can be a good way to build empathy (the ability to imagine how others are feeling).

• Keep a box of objects that can be used to help prevent, or recover from, a meltdown — beanbags to pummel and throw around, an old saucepan to beat, bubbles to blow to help regulate breathing, etc.

Go online

Visit Usborne Quicklinks for links to websites with more tips on how to encourage young children to explore and talk about their feelings, and activities and video clips to share with them.

Go to www.usborne.com/quicklinks and type in the keywords 'all about feelings'. Please read our internet safety guidelines at the Usborne Quicklinks website. We recommend children are supervised online.